All My Naked Soul

An original collection of poems exploring the complexities of living with a mental illness.

Patricia J. Morris

O&U

Onwards & Upwards

Onwards and Upwards Publishers

3 Radfords Turf

Cranbrook

Exeter

EX5 7DX

United Kingdom

www.onwardsandupwards.org

First edition, published in the United Kingdom by Onwards and Upwards Publishers Ltd. (2019).

ISBN: 978-1-78815-544-1
Typeface: Sabon LT
Graphic design: LM Graphic Design

Printed in the United Kingdom.

About the Author

Patricia Morris grew up in North London as part of a large, boisterous family. Her love of reading and writing were always her way of finding quiet times amidst the noise. Patricia understood very early that her way of expressing herself, her experiences and her faith was going to be through writing poetry.

Her first experience of success was writing a Christmas carol for her school choir at the age of twelve and then winning a prize in a National Writing Competition run by the African-Caribbean Education Resource Project (ACER) aged sixteen.

Patricia continued to be a prolific writer; writing songs and plays for her local church. However, she kept much of her poetry private until she an opportunity to speak at a women's event. There she found that her poetry was not only a true reflection of herself, but also able to give a voice to the unspoken experience of many who live with mental health issues.

Endorsement

For the last seven years Patricia has been invited to participate as a speaker in the Chosen Ministry Women's Day Program and each year it is with great anticipation that we look forward to what she has to share. Many of the women who attend this program are fans of Patricia's thought-provoking poetry, and with good reason

Her poetry has the ability to touch the secret places within without feeling judgement; there is a deep empathy in Patricia's poems. They are engaging and compelling and lovely and sad in equal measure. There is also a feeling of victory even though that may not always be obvious; however, if you can just hang on to the next page you will be able to feel hope through her words, her phases, her seasons and experiences.

The fact that Patricia is able to be so transparent is a rare quality and makes her even more beautiful; she is passionate, deliberate, a champion of many; she is brave.

She speaks her truth, which is both piercing and delicate at the same time, and no matter where you are in life's journey or where you come from, there are elements of her poetry that one can identify with. At our times of deepest reflection, we acknowledge that we have much more in common than we care to realise as her poetry shines the light on some of our untold stories, our unshared pain and the masked areas of our lives. We are fans because Patricia, through her poetry, tells our truth.

I am both honoured and humbled to endorse *My Naked Soul* – an inspirational, courageous and timely must-read book of poetry.

Christine Oteh
Chosen Women Fellowship

To all the amazing women in my life who have
helped me on this journey.

To my mother, Enid Morgan, for her persistent love
and prayers;

to the Chosen Women Ministry at Westbury
Avenue Baptist Church, where I first found, and
continue to find, my authentic voice;

and to Grace Chimwe and Eluria Morgan for their
unwavering, unstinted friendship and belief in me.

Contents

Foreword by Dr Esther Fenty

The experience of being a Christian in a hostile environment and the struggle that presents is one that resonates with every Christian. However, this book goes beyond that type of warfare and explores through poetry the 'elephant in the room'; the unacknowledged mental health conditions that are present among many Christians who suffer in pain, loneliness and silence. In *All My Naked Soul*, Patricia Morris takes up the challenge to write not only about the subject but about her personal experience in dealing with a medical condition and the accompanying mental health issues of anxiety and panic attacks. She refuses to hide behind the veil of Christian platitudes and bares her soul firstly to God poignantly and through her writing allows the reader to share the truth of her experience.

The rollercoaster of Patricia's emotions that are captured within her poetry means that there could not be a more fitting title for this book than *All My Naked Soul*. The title of the book is intriguing as the reader wonders what will be revealed in a 'naked soul'; darkness or enlightenment, sadness or happiness, joy or sorrow, bondage or freedom? Through her exploration of these and many more themes, Patricia traces her journey in poetry in three stages from turmoil to triumph. At each stage, there is a candidness that will resonate with Christians with a mental health condition but also those facing some adversity of any kind. Like the Apostle Paul who explained in 1 Corinthians 9:16 that he was compelled to preach the gospel, so Patricia's poem in the prelude indicates that she is compelled to write. The themes of loneliness, pain, bewilderment of the turmoil, hopelessness and panic attacks are vividly portrayed during the first stage. There is a progression through surrender in Stage 2 but accompanied by spiritual warfare, crying behind closed doors and an acknowledgment of prayer warriors who help us on the journey. Finally, there is triumph through pain as Patricia's faith in Jesus becomes stronger and she is able to offer hope and encouragement to others.

Struggling with a mental health condition is not easy, especially when it is clouded in silence within our churches. Throughout the book, the reader glimpses not only some of Patricia's suffering but her faith in God's ability to walk alongside her through every situation that she faces and bring her into victory. Through her acceptance of God's continual presence with her, she is able to find God in the darkness of pain and experience liberation. Patricia did not allow suffering to reject God but her faith in God has played an enormous part in her healing and writing has been her outlet. Her writings demonstrate the truth of 2 Corinthians 4:16: "Therefore we do not give up. Even though our outer person is being destroyed, our inner person is being renewed day by day."

This book is for those who have suffered in silence; believing that they are all alone and no one understands them. It is for those who are at any stage of their mental health or spiritual journey and it gives hope that inner healing is possible. This book is borne out of Patricia's experience of pain and having known and worked alongside her in ministry for many years, I can attest to this. Patricia Morris is a gifted, talented, creative communicator, writer and teacher. She is a committed Christian who despite her suffering is faithful in her work with children and young people both in her local church and nationally.

I invite you to read this insightful book of poetry which depicts mental health suffering through the lens of Patricia Morris. You will find revelations which identify with your Christian journey and struggles; whether it is sickness, loss, mental or physical well-being. This book of poetry encourages you to trust in God as submission to Him brings liberation. In so doing, you will find what St Augustine confessed centuries ago, "You have made us for yourself, O Lord, and our hearts are restless until they can find rest in you."

Prelude

But the woman, fearing and trembling, knowing what was done in her, came and fell down before him, and told him all the truth.

Mark 5:33

I HAVE A MENTAL HEALTH CONDITION. IT HAS A NAME. I can explain the simple science of what it is and why it occurs. I don't mean to 'claim it' like my brown eyes and my black hair, but like those things, it is intrinsically part of me. Unlike those things, it has a direct effect on how I live my life. It colours my interactions with people. It changes how I connect with a place, person or situation at a given time. Not speaking about it does not make it less real. Not saying it makes it that much harder to live with. Not saying it means I must find ways to hide and disguise it. I have spent a great deal of my life learning how to hide it, disguise it, prevent the world from seeing it. Yet, through my poetry I have seen how my soul has found its own way of declaring its truth. For anyone who chooses to read, the struggle of my soul spills out on to the paper.

Writing is at once a learnt skill and a natural organic experience. For as long as I can remember, I wrote words; in poetry, songs, short stories and diaries. I made up stories in my head and lived them in my mind. In the world I created, I was all at once beautiful, free, successful, loved and loving, creative, real and magical. In gatherings where I often felt out of step, out of place and out of sync, I could disappear into the words in my head. I could be present and absent all at once. I could be unknown and untouchable. In situations where I was forced to confront reality without that shield, I would be overwhelmed, scared, nervous, anxious. After those events, I would spend days aching and tired. I did not understand then, as I understand now, that my system, both physically and neurologically, was overwhelmed and the shutdown was its way of renewing itself.

As a Christian, mental health is a difficult subject. For those of us who suffer, we often find it challenging to speak our truth. From my experience, most people's understanding of mental illness is of the extreme: the man in the street who talks to himself; the woman who is unkempt; strange public behaviours that are not the 'norm'. It conjures up the image of the man in the Bible afflicted with demons; violent and uncontrollable.

For many people, to say "I have" in relation to any medical condition, let alone a mental health condition, is to claim its power over them and to deny the power and authority of the Almighty God. I have been corrected again and again if I use the pronoun 'my' in relation to my physical and mental health. I have been told that the condition does not belong to me. It is not mine. Whilst it may not be my condition, it is my truth; and for me, healing can only come when we speak our truth, without fear and without reservation.

In Mark 5:25-34 we find the account of the woman with the issue of blood. In secret she had sought doctors and medics to no avail. Because of her condition, she would have been isolated, shunned, ashamed. Her flow of blood made her unclean and unfit for society. She had to live in the shadows of life. When she went into the crowd to touch Jesus, her thought was just to touch the hem of His garment and then creep away in secrecy and shame. But when Jesus acknowledged her, we are told in verse 33 that she "fell down before Him and told Him all the truth". It is then that Jesus says to her, "Daughter, thy faith has made thee whole; go in peace and be whole of thy plague."

By telling Jesus "all the truth", she was not just healed physically. Jesus gave her peace; a freedom from her shame, her insecurity, her isolation.

Life is not always as we would wish it. The race we run in life is a story of triumph and failure; highs and lows. We must begin to tell all the truth about our conditions in life, no matter the stigma or the shame. If we live in the shadows, ashamed, hidden and disguised, how can we tell all our truth? How can our testimony have any significance if we do not reveal our whole story? How can someone be lifted, encouraged, by the love, light and healing of God if they do not understand the journey to our victory; if they do not see the race we have run? How can we overcome if we do not tell all our truth?

This, then, is "all my truth". This is all my naked soul, in struggle, in loss, in victory.

All My Naked Soul

When I sit down to write
I find that my heart has leaked from the tip of my pen.
I look down on to the formerly pure, blank page
to see all my naked soul laid bare for the reader's eye.
I cannot cover it up,
I cannot clothe it in fig-leaved robes of anonymity.
Too late.
For the words have become life
    and whisper my deep silence
to wandering eyes that care to read between the lines.

When the mood to compose overwhelms me
I look down to find that the thoughts that creep and mist
around the edges of my mind
have stained the virgin purity of the page
so that every prying eye can read
    the sorrow of my longing.
The words have become a voice that I do not recognise,
shouting secrets that I never knew.
I cannot hide them under a bushel.
I cannot force them back into the dark.
Oh no.
For they have become a light
    that leads every curious reader
to the very essence of me.

When the jumble in my mind becomes words
I look down to find that my pen
    has scratched out deviant verse
that corrupts the once innocent page
so that learned readers can infer the reality of my being.
The words have become like wandering sheep,
    scattering my joy
and echoing my sins over every hill.

I cannot herd them back;
I cannot command them.
Oh no.
For they have strayed into the minds of all those who care
to read the book of my captured soul.

Human Race

I don't remember signing up;
    I did not hear the starter's gun
Yet, I find myself competing
    in a never-ending run
I've been told that at the finishing line
    a prize waits for me
And I have no choice but to run this race
    to wherever it may lead

So, I strap my identity to my back,
    gear up and take my place
To become a fierce competitor
    in this timeless, endless race
A gentle breeze lifts me on to
    a long and narrow road
My zeal and my enthusiasm spur me
    on to the unknown

There are no cheering spectators
    to line the long, long road
But each one is a competitor
    and must run on alone
For a little while another soul
    joins with me in the race
We run on together
    as our hearts and feet keep pace
But as quickly as the melting snow
    and the setting sun
They disappear without a trace
    and I am left alone to run

I am running through mysteries,
          through secrets and through lies
Through joys that seem to quickly pass,
          through tears and smiles and sighs
I run through disappointments,
          the many breakings of my heart
I run despite the arrows,
          the slings, the fiery darts

I run through love, I run through hate;
          I run through pain and grief
I run through times of battle;
          I run through times of peace
Yet the promised horizon
          seems further still away
And I pray through all my running
          that I will not run in vain

I am running and I'm running
          and I am running faster still
Though my breath rips in exhaustion
          I possess an iron will
A soul-deep determination
          to complete what I've begun
Though before there's no horizon
          and behind no setting sun
Just an endless trail of doubts and fears
          that keep snapping at my heels
And shadows upon shadows
          that surround me like old trees
That refuse to obey commandments
          and are deaf to all my pleas
And the drumbeats of my footsteps
          are pounding loud and clear
As I'm desperate to outrun them,
          but they stay forever near

As I'm running and I'm running,
    and my body feels the strain
I wish that I could stop awhile
    and that someone would explain
Why something deep within me
    that I do not understand
Persuades me to keep running
    to that distant Promised Land

With no stopping or no slowing
    in this race of endless time
There is a fear that now propels me
    towards this mystery prize
And I'm running and I'm running
    with hope and with despair
For though I know that I will reach it,
    what it is, is never clear

I've heard tales whispered on the winds
    of those who left the race
How they fell like leaves at autumn
    and were trodden in disgrace
I cannot let that be my fate,
    for I have given this race my all
I have sacrificed all that I am;
    my heart, my life, my soul

And I when I am resigned to be
    running forever more
I see somewhere beyond me,
    a gleaming, distant shore
Where a waving band of people
    seem to beam at me with pride
As they beckon and encourage me
    to sprint to the other side

So, I'm running and I'm running
        and I'm running toward the line
That marks the bitter-sweet completion
        of this race of endless time
Though I'm weary and I'm tired
        and I'm glad the end's in sight
I wonder what I'll do now,
        without the race that's been my life

Then I'm lifted by a sense of joy,
        as if on angel's wings
And hear that merry band of people
        begin to celebrate and sing
For another long-distance runner
        has finally made it through
And a sense of peace within me
        springs forth like morning dew
My weary feet alight on that
        sacred Promised Land
And I become one with that chorus;
        that singing, joyful band

Then sweeping through the singing,
        like the cool of the evening air
I hear the voice of someone speaking to me
        loud and clear
The voice echoes with calm authority,
        as if it knew my heart
As it begins to tell my journey
        right from the very start
As the details of my race
        seem to move before my eyes
I wonder if I am worthy
        to receive that longed-for prize
I wonder how I had made it;
        and how I had survived

When I see how much I stumbled;
    I see the anger and the strain
I tremble at the thought that
    I might be made to start again

But with beautiful reassurance
    the voice comes to my ears
And says, "For you the race is over,
    the grief the pain, the tears
For though your run was not perfect,
    I know you gave your best
Come now and claim your prize
    Lie down
    and sleep
    and rest."

ACT ONE

My Soul in Turmoil

It is not in me ... God shall give an answer of peace.

Genesis 41:16

THE BRAIN IS A COMPLEX MACHINE. LIKE ANY MACHINE, when there is a disruption in the way it works, it causes a malfunction. When the mind is disrupted by mental illness, it causes a disruption in the soul. A disrupted soul is a soul that is not at peace. When I am not a peace, I feel constantly that I am on shaky ground. When my soul is in turmoil, I try to find ways of covering it up – I retreat; I avoid; I hide behind formality and professionalism – until I can find ways of reasserting my sense of peace. I do not want people to see my soul in turmoil. I feel ashamed and anxious that I will be judged, that I will be seen as falling short of what God and others require of me. I think people will see me as someone who does not have enough faith in God – because, after all, "God has not given us the spirit of fear; but of power, and of love, and of a sound mind" (2 Tim. 1:7).

So, I put those layers of lies over my struggle and those lies have formed a great deal of the impression people have of me: I'm shy; I'm quiet; I'm antisocial; I don't like people; I'm a loner; I'm very 'independent'; I don't like to ask for help; I'm stubborn. Anyone who knows me at all will have said or heard one of these things about me. The truth is, being with people I don't know makes me feel anxious and unsure, so I say very little until I can establish firm footing.

Being in large crowds, with lots of noise, overwhelms my senses; my 'flight or fight' reflexes kick in and I feel panicked – I want to run away. Sometimes, all it takes is some quiet time alone to readjust and I am fine. For example, when I have been teaching all morning, I don't go to the staffroom at lunchtime, because my brain is overwhelmed and I need time alone to come back to myself so I can teach in the afternoon. Without that time, my anxiety worsens. I have panic attacks that sweep over me from nowhere.

In those times, God in His infinite wisdom allows words to slip out of my mind and on to the page. For a long time, I was uncomfortable with some of those words. They did not seem to express what a child of God should feel. Why would a God-fearing, Bible-believing Christian write words of loss, anger, hopelessness, fear and panic? Why have I given voice to those feelings, rather than rebuke them, deny them, shun them?

Those words are part of my truth – they are the reality of my life. They are the voices of the chaos of my mind that I live with; that I must overcome every day in order to worship, work, form friendships, maintain my life beyond the walls of my mind. And I do overcome. Not because of anything that *I* can do. The answer of peace in those times of chaos is not in me. Every day that I can maintain a life full of things that so many people take for granted, it is a battle won. But the war is continuous and there are days when I lose the battle. There are days when the chaos in my mind wins and it is hard to bear.

A soul in turmoil is a soul at odds with itself. I am aware of God's peace and His ability to soothe my soul, but in those times when anxiety and panic win, that peace is lost. I struggle with the dichotomy of who I am and how I want to appear, with the chaos of a mind that is overwhelmed. But through it all, whether I am able to grasp it in that moment or not, I know that the answer of peace is not within me.

God often gave prophets words to voice their pain – to give voice to those times when the peace of their soul was disrupted. David, Job and Elijah all gave voice to the instability of their mind in different seasons. In Psalm 88:3 David says, "...my soul is full of troubles: and my life draweth nigh unto the grave." In verse 6 of the same psalm, he asserts, "Thou hast laid me in the lowest pit, in darkness, in the deeps." Job, in Job 6:11, echoes what I sometimes feel when my soul is in turmoil: "What is my strength that I should hope? and what is my end that I should prolong my life?" There are times like Elijah in 1 Kings 19:4 when I feel that I cannot go on and say, "It is enough; now O Lord, take my life." It is through this honest confession of weakness that we can see the victory of God over the chaos that can sometimes take hold in our minds. When we acknowledge that we are weak and come to the end of ourselves, we can also acknowledge that the answer of peace is not within us. These servants of the Lord looked to God to give the answer of peace, to soothe the soul, to hold it safe in the times of storm, and restore it.

You may find some of the poems in this section uncomfortable reading; you may might find that they act as a trigger, in which case there is help available, and support numbers can be found in the Appendix, should you need them. You may find that they are words that resonate with you – you may recognise your own turmoil, or the turmoil of a loved one or friend. It is okay to acknowledge that turmoil, to name it, to understand that your soul is experiencing a disruption of peace. In those days when I cannot seem to find my way through the darkness, God gives an answer of peace and restores me.

My Heart

My Heart
That delicate hypochondriac
Shrinks from every tender embrace
In fear of attack from fatal emotion

My Heart
That shy and tender thing
Sleeps in its protective cocoon
To avoid the sharp sting of reality

My Heart
Fears what it does not know
But runs from knowledge with Olympic dedication
To take succour in its own loneliness

My Heart
That flawed and fragile being
Beats and cries; beats and cries
In an endless rhythm of caged hypocrisy

The Introvert's Prayer

There are times when I need
To be alone with myself
Away from the constant chatter of the world
Away from the endless doling out of
      pieces of myself for hire
Away from being expected, or anticipated or waited for
To stop the endless vain spinning of time
Rushing me nowhere
So that each tick of the clock belongs only to me

There are times when I want to run away
From the platitudes that ask but do not listen
Away from a wanted smile
When tears are required
Away from babbling conversation
When a bubbling stream of repressed pain wants to erupt

But to be; just me
As weak or strong as I choose
When I choose
Not to be comforted
Not to have to get over or get through
To wallow
If wallowing is my pointless pleasure

Not to be talent or wisdom or creation
To not exist
If non-existence is possible for one brief space of time
Not to be known or understood
Not to be Woman or Friend or Teacher or Lover
But to have my own name
To see myself through my own eyes
Through my own mirror
To be only and only me

My own self-portrait
With no other artistic interpretation

Not to be endlessly poured out, wrung out, dried out
Not to be pulled and stretched beyond my possibility
Until I am empty and spent and shattered and soul-less

But time
To retreat inside myself
So that I can be myself
Come back to myself
Give me back to me
To be whole again
Before it begins again

Bitter Embers

You think I give a flying fig
When you take and take but do not give;
Until my empty shell is in the dirt
Gasping, drowning in my thirst?
I just lick my teeth and swallow spit
And say, well, that's just the way of it.
You think I care? You think I'm bothered
That all my darling dreams were smothered?
Like a baby born into slavery
Better dead, than not living free.
I am not bent, and I am not bowed
When faced with the jeering of the crowd:
Their words don't hurt, and their lies don't sting.
In fact, I don't feel anything.
I do not hope, and I do not pine
You cannot say I'm not feeling fine.
I'm never broke and I'm never poor
They never leave me wanting more.
Late at night, when terror hovers
Like my only constant lover;
You think I scream aloud in fear
And wish that there were someone near?
No! I clench my fists and face the fright.
I shadowbox till morning light.
You think my faith in you is blighted?
It was never there. I'm not disappointed
That all my comrades have fled the fray
And I am left alone to pay.
When all that's in me is spent and gone
My strength depleted, my courage none
I will not break or succumb to pain
Because I know that I must rise again.

Panic Attack

I exhale
deeply
and expel all my fears

Only to breathe them in again
with my next breath

I feel the stench of them taint
my nostrils

Each breath
is an exercise in control;
a battle I am gradually losing

The oxygen around me is full
of unseen terrors;
a shadow
of a shadow
that is tangible only to me

Each breath
is an
exercise in control;
a ledge
from which I am gradually
slipping

I cannot
hold on
to your reality

Real to me
is that edge of a nightmare
that pulls me into a familiar
hell

Each
breath
is an exercise
in control;
a race that
I am
gradually losing

The words in my head are
Babel,
strange languages that just
confuse me;
I am not sure
what I am
saying

And I cannot hear you

Each
b-r-e-a-t-h
is an
exercise in
control

My control is breaking

My skin is alien to me
It is like yellow wallpaper
I want to strip it and let the
demons out

I want to
cry
but the tears pool like acid in
my gut

I want to
scream
but I am afraid of where the
sound will take me

I want
to
let
go

to
shatter,
to fall
apart

Each
breath
is
an
exercise
in
control

Unsung Blues

An unsung blues is a pain so deep
It makes grown men wail and women weep.
An unsung blues is a pain so wide
It forms a chasm deep inside.

An unsung blues is a silent scream;
A visible wound that remains unseen.
An unsung blues is a constant pain
That bleeds and heals; then bleeds again.

This unsung blues wants to erupt
In fits and bursts and shorts and struts
To break the bars of its minim cage
And bleed its bile across this page.

My unsung blues yearns to be free
To sing its song and let me be me
To split its wrists and joy to find
That hell is real; but God is kind.

This blues wants to escape my pen
To tell its truth in rage and then
Use that sword to pierce my soul
Till me and blues and life are whole.

If I had the chance to sing my blues
I'd tell it like it was bitter news
And maybe if I had the chance to sing
I wouldn't say a single thing.

Loss

There is a constant pain inside of me
That within my body and soul resides
That can somehow always still remind me
That of all the dreams I have put aside
You'll always remain that frequent shadow
That torments my life with what might have been
And I recognise that each tomorrow
Will tell your absence with every scene
I can find no dream that will surpass you
No earthly or heavenly pleasures fill
That deepest void you've left behind you
I cannot seem to find the strength of will
To close forever in a cold dark tomb
The bitter sorrow of a fruitless womb.

Hopeless

There was a time
Once upon a time
When dreams were in my reach
I thought I could stretch and pluck them from the sky
With unfeigned unchained belief
In some charmed and blessed naïveté
I thought I could scale every wall

But...

I don't believe in miracles anymore.

There was a time
Once upon a time
When all my hope was spring
That grew and flowed in endless waves
Like some heavenly song they sing
Wondrously, I believed
That I would become My All

But...

I don't believe in miracles anymore.

There came a time
Once upon a time
When truth came home to rest
It took up residence in my hope
And crushed my dreams to death
So that the sweetest nectar of my God
Became a bitter gall
And I can't believe in miracles anymore.

Life and Death

I am sure death is easier
Than these endlessly stretching to nothing days
These flowing and floating in nothing days
These mindless living for nothing days

I am sure death is more certain
Than these always on shaky ground days
These rug pulled out from your dreams days
These trembling and tumbling of heart days

I am sure death is kinder
Than these waking struggling for breath days
These frightened of life beyond doors days
These edge and end of insane days

I am sure death is sweeter
Than these longing and lingering beyond hope days
These flickerings of dubious joy days
These losing again and again days

I am sure death is purer
Than these praying for heaven and home days
These singing and wishing for glory days
These soon I will be done with the world days

These days
These blue and broken days
These token of life days
When nothing is bright days
Can only end in death
And sweeter and kinder and purer days.

After-Death

When I was dead; when I died
The people came, the people cried
They said those things, those things they said
When I died, when I was dead
They sang the songs – those songs they sing
They brought the grief that people bring
They spoke of love; those people who
Came to mourn my passing through
The love I had; the love I gave
Does love pass beyond the grave?
They knew me well, the people said
Before I died; before I was dead
They never knew about the fears
That dogged my soul through blackened years
They could not know; I never said
The people claimed when I was dead
Those people prayed and hung their heads
When I died; when I was dead
To comfort those I left behind
For those who mourned and those who cried
They prayed their peace upon my soul
Though they did not know where it had gone

Jazz

a blue sun rose above my window
that seemed to cast my day in doubt
and piercing through the lurid sunshine
the yellow bluebirds seemed to shout
"stay to slumber
sleep to die
tell your heart no reasons why"
but i have not yet been defeated
i am not yet cast away
stop the yellow mist from falling
let lovers cry for yesterday

a blood red path beneath my footsteps
leads me to a place unknown
yet i have followed bleaker rainbows
to find that which i can call my own
from jagged hilltops
ravaged pride
there's nowhere left for me to hide
for i will not be shut in silence
i have not held hope at bay
it pulls me from the miry shadows
let lovers cry for yesterday

ACT TWO

My Soul in Faith

The Lord is nigh unto them that are of a broken heart; and saveth such as be of a contrite spirit.

Psalm 34:18

I REMEMBER BACK TO WHEN I MADE THE DECISION TO fully surrender my life to the God. I had been going to church regularly for several years, after a lengthy absence, but I always put off that final surrender because I knew that to live truly the way God wanted me to live, I would have to walk away from some things and some people in my life. In the end though, it wasn't a difficult decision. I got to a point where I could no longer ignore the calling from God.

In the week leading up to my baptism and the weeks afterwards, I felt a freedom and a peace that were indescribable. I felt so much lighter and so calm in myself. In the years since that decision, I have never regretted it nor wanted my old way of life back. But, I cannot say that I have always felt that same sense of peace or freedom.

Life happens. The first thing was that after several years of absence, panic attacks returned, seemingly out of nowhere. For one of the first times in my life I was content and happy, and suddenly, I found myself having panic attacks. I could not understand nor explain the reasons for them. My bouts of anxiety and low mood became more frequent. I would find myself sad for no reason, less social, less willing to be a part of things. Then there was the pain. I had always had periods when I would be in so much pain I did not know what to do with myself. These become more frequent and more prolonged. There was no real explanation for them. I would feel completely tired and wiped out, for no reason. My work began to suffer. I could not explain the reasons for the pain, and nothing I did or the doctor did made it go away. This made the anxiety and depression worse. There were times when I thought I was going mad. I had X-rays and two laparoscopies, all of which showed nothing. It felt as though it was all in my head. At the same time, I felt a weight

41

of expectation, from my work, from my church, from my family. I hardly went to any large family events, and it was so hard to explain that I was tired or sick, or feeling so anxious there was no way I would be able to get on a train or drive myself on the motorway. It was hard to make anyone understand, because I didn't really understand myself.

Being diagnosed with Fibromyalgia and Panic/Anxiety Disorder gave a name to what I was suffering; but there is no cure and treatments work sporadically. I have had to try to tailor my life around chronic pain, fatigue, anxiety and depression. It has, and it continues to be, a struggle every day. Apart from the daily pain, I grieve for the person I was, and I grieve for the person I can no longer be.

Through it all, I have tried to hold on to my faith and my belief in God. There are times in my faith journey when I feel so connected to that faith, so connected to the word, so connected to who I am in Christ and who Christ is in my life. But there have been also times when I have felt so abandoned by God. I have never stopped believing in Him, but I sometimes doubt His power in my life. I know that I am still here because of His power in my life, even when I cannot grasp it. On those days I used to struggle with feelings of guilt and shame. I had listened to all the testimonies of people who had gone through horrendous times, and through it all they had 'held on to God's unchanging hand'. I felt guilty because I felt I could not do that.

But God is faithful. He understands those times of doubt and fear. He never really leaves me alone. In those times, God will always find a way to bring me back to Him, to help to restore my faith and hope and trust in who He is and what He has planned for my life. God hears my cry when I am in despair; when the pain or anxiety becomes so unbearable that I feel lost. He hears my moans, and He hears the words that I do not or cannot utter. He knows when I am feeling lost and adrift and, like a loving shepherd, He comes to seek me and bring me back to His fold.

I wish I could always be on the mountaintop; I wish I could always hold on to that serenity that I first found when I took that step to surrender. I wish there were no valleys to walk through. The scriptures say, "Yea though I walk through the valley of the shadow of death..." (Psalm 23:4) so we know that there will be low times. But it goes on to say, "...thou art with me; thy rod and thy staff, they comfort me." I thank God that in those times He still sees me; He still sees my worth, even when I feel worthless. He has hope for me when I feel hopeless. In those times when my past haunts me and my future seems so uncertain and hopeless, God finds a way to remind me of His love and I live on and carry on in His strength alone.

The pain and the anxiety and the depression still happen. The days of feeling lost and adrift still happen. But in the midst of it all, God is there; through the peaks and the valleys, God is there; through the good and the bad, God is there. Through it all, He keeps me in His hands and reminds me that I am His, until I can once again believe it for myself.

Faith is not static. Faith is a living, growing thing. It can be weakened and strengthened by our life's experiences. Through it all, God is still God and I am still His child, and when I am lost, He finds ways to remind me that I am His and He is mine.

Surrender

Today
I have decided
I am going to step over the edge of the precipice
I am going to leap toward that voice
    that has been calling me

And yet...
My pain smiles
And my fears comfort me with their familiarity
I have been here before
Wavering
Uncertain

But, today
I am going to take that last step over the edge
Into the thing I know is waiting

And yet...
My past haunts me
Bays
Calls at me
Draws me in like sin

And I am tempted

But...

There is a still, small voice
Beckoning me over
Bidding me come

So, today
I put one foot out
Certain

Sure again
And yet...
My abuse jeers
"You will never be free of me
My chains are bound around your heart"
It clutches at my back
And holds me...

Until...

I hear the still small voice
Beckoning me over
Bidding me come
And I step
Freefall
Feel His arms surround me
Mid-air
And I know.

The Sinner's Mourning

These thirty pieces of silver
Cannot wash away my sin
These thirty pieces of silver
Cannot cleanse this guilty stain
They cannot buy redemption
Or satisfy my soul
They cannot buy my peace of mind
They cannot make me whole

This silver cannot dry my tears
Nor stop my aching heart
They cannot rebuild this shattered life
My greed has torn apart
In their vulgar glitter
There is no beauty, joy or truth
But bitter condemnation
Betrayal, guilt and blood

Yet in that man called Jesus
All beauty and grace is found
And for our sins the innocent lamb
Is sold to a bleating, baying crowd
And these thirty pieces of silver
Will never match the price
That Jesus paid just for me
In His final sacrifice

Spiritual Warfare

They tell me the past has passed
That it's time to let it go at last
I turn this thought over in my mind
And try to find the truth of it
Then I can pluck out the root of the fear
That has always hounded me
Wrapped my heart in chains and bound me
I try to do as they say; let it all go
Let it all drift away
They say it's only a matter of time, prayer and patience
As time tick-tocks, I pray the Psalm of David
How long, O Lord, how long
Will I have this stronghold over me?
How long, O Lord, wilt thou forsake me?
And I wait, and I wait; my soul doth wait
I try to heed what they say; let it all go
Let it all melt away
But every time I think I shake it
It comes back harder, stronger and I just can't take it
The flow is a flood and I am once again naked
Another wave hits me; I'm smarting and burning
This weapon of self-destruction seems to be working
Lord, please, I need your banner of protection
I'm drowning in this spiritual insurrection
Overwhelmed by emotion, I can't seem to hold on
I need an altar to lay my grief on
Still they say, let it go, He is with you
But I can't feel His presence
My heart is enclosed behind a high wall of loneliness
As hard as I try, I can't seem to scale it
I've tried to explain it, but they don't understand
They think that my longing is just for some man
To rescue me, or complete me;
They think I need someone to reveal the joys of sex to me

But I've tried that solution; it doesn't work, it's just work
Flesh on flesh does not make you whole
I need something that will feed my soul
Because I really can't live on bread alone
But, they say, let it go
The battle's not yours, it belongs to the Lord
But here I am; dying yet fighting
The savage within me still clawing and biting
Though I'm hurt and scared and battle-weary
I'm bleeding and screaming;
  why doesn't somebody hear me?
Am I whispering too loud, drowned out by the crowd?
A host of invisible ghosts that suffocate and surround me
And I'm down on my knees and I'm pleading
Lord, please, please, take away this thorn
That's piercing my side, my soul, my gut
Cos whatever I have just isn't enough
And I can't let it go, I can't, don't you see?
I don't know how to release this pressure inside me
That builds and builds until I think I'll explode
Or implode, internally, eternally wounded
Slain by the thought that I just can't get through it
Let it go, let it go, they say, don't you know
The monster that created your demons is no more
He's RIP; so, we suggest it's best, if you just let it be
But where is my calm, my promised peace
Maybe it will only come with that sweet release
Maybe the final conclusion
Will be to tip the ledge and fall into this ball of confusion
So that the I in me is dead; and instead
The swirl of insanity in my mind
  is the only way I find to exist
Though, I think before it comes to this

I need to let it go

Behind Closed Doors

Behind closed doors
There's the sound of my weeping
Pregnant with the pain I've been concealing
As hard as I try, I just can't give birth to it
So, I hide it
Wrap it up tight and bind it.
And every day I repair
The mask that I wear
Only by God's grace am I standing here

Behind closed doors
I am like Hannah
Pouring out my grief on my own private altar
Whilst I wrestle with the demons I'm trying to slaughter
And the fight is brutal
So, my steps sometimes falter

In the midst of the sanctuary
I dance out my praise
Because behind closed doors
I devour page after page of the word
Until it's seeped into my spirit
Until I can crawl into its strength
And worship within it

Behind closed doors
My faith waivers
My prayers stutter like Tourette's
Nonsensical words
That only the love and mercy of God could have heard
And how He took them and used them
I can't understand
So, I don't try
I just lift my hands,

Marvel at the grace that covers me
That's taking this rocking ship and keeping it steady

Behind closed doors
I'm drifting into a wide-open sea
Where waves of temptation want to overwhelm me
Until a still small voice brings me safe to the shore
And I'm anchored safe in the love of Jesus once more

Behind closed doors
My strength is depleted
But my phone is ringing because somebody needs me
I show up to do what I have to do
Because behind closed doors
God came through
So that the me that you get is not the me that I was
But the me that is reflecting the love of God

Behind closed doors
When I am weak and I'm tired
My soul sings Psalms
Until I am inspired by the Word
        to create words of my own
To worship the saviour that sits on the throne
King of my life
My abiding joy
Faithful though my doubts sometimes
        crowd out His voice

Behind closed doors
I feel all alone
Loneliness grips me like a dart to my soul
He shows up in my solitude and calls me His own
And gives me a purpose
A reason to be
To step from the shadows
With strength to believe

That all that I will, and all that I am
Is cradled gently in His mighty hand
Don't mistake my praise for a life without struggle
It's just that behind closed doors
God comes in and fights every battle
And I can live safe and secure
Because God is still God behind closed doors.

The Persistent Storm

I have a storm that will not pass;
Even though I've prayed,
The promised answer of my faith
Seems very much delayed.
I long to hear, "Peace, be still!"
And for the waves to calm,
But in the silence, rain I hear
And my storm lingers on.
The storm clouds hover ever above;
They let no daylight through
But threaten me with darker days
That suddenly come true.
I strain to hear, "Peace, be still!"
But all I hear is thunder
And each angry shout of the sky
Tears my hope asunder.
The devastation of the storm
Seems to have no abating
It wreaks its havoc on my soul
And leads my faith to fainting.
Though I hear not, "Peace, be still!"
I feel the hand of God.
My ravaged soul rests in His arms
As my storm lingers on.

Ecclesiastes

When the season
Has stripped their leaves bare
And they stand, naked and unashamed
I sit and admire their boldness

Branches still stretched upwards
Reaching in praise to their God

They are undaunted by
The sudden onset of cruelty
That has lain to waste their beauty

Branches still upright
Swaying in Psalm song to their God

When the burden of winter snow
Weighs heavily on them
They are not bowed low

Branches still stretched high
In reverence to their mighty God

I am awed by their faith
Their simple certainty
That spring will come once more
To renew them

Can I too,
Stripped bare in autumn pain and winter silence,
Stand boldly naked
Arms stretched upwards in praise
Reaching for my God?

Can Psalm song still sway my heart?

Can I stand sure
In simple, certain faith
Knowing that whatever the seasons bring
Spring will come once more
To renew me?

Not by Bread Alone

The scripture tells us that in this world
Whether faced with joy or sorrow
We must call on the Word
So when I am weak and my faith almost gone
The Lord God whispers, "Not by bread alone."

Not by bread alone
Is the song I sing in the face of temptation
Knowing that my constant source of inspiration
Comes not from the world
But from every word
That proceeds from the mouth of God

Not by bread alone
Means comfort in the wilderness of my fears
So even when the enemy jeers, my constant guide
The Living Word is on my side
The Living Word – Jesus Christ

Not by bread alone
Is my soul's delight, keeps me armed for the fight
So that when the enemy roars
I just lift up the sword of righteousness
And rebuke the mess he tries to make of my life
The Sword, the Living Word, Jesus Christ

Not by bread alone
Tells me I can let go, and not pursue
The things that will lead me from the truth
Because of His sacrifice,
The Bread of Heaven, who laid down His life
Looking to the hills from whence comes my help
My life, my God, my righteousness

Yes, I walk in victory
I have the seal of my Lord upon me
I walk on solid ground now that I have found
The way, the truth, the life
The Living Word, Jesus Christ
The enemy tries to baffle me, confuse me, tempt me
This fallen world tries to ensnare me
Tries to twist the Word and make me falter
Wants me to stumble and waver,
But I know that I am strong
Because I do not live by bread alone

The Praying Mother

When all the house is sleeping
The weary sun is sinking low
When the silent night comes creeping
And the stars begin to glow:
The rush of day has ended
And the sweetest dreams, they linger near
Then Almighty God, whom she befriended
Inclines His ear to hear
A mother's earnest prayers
Carried through the night-time sky
As she casts all her trials and cares
Unto Him who sits on high.
She thanks the Lord Almighty
With a grateful heart
For the children, in blood and spirit
And the joy that they impart.
She petitions Him with silent tears
That He would hold them close
To all that she's taught them through the years
Of the glory of the cross.
She prays that they will not stray
Too far, too late, from God
That they will always know the name
Of the One who calmed the flood.
She prays the songs she sang them
When in their cradle resting
Will recall to them their hiding place
While in their days of testing.
Her heart breaks when their hearts break
And she prays to the One who loves them
That He will their grief and sorrow take
And in love and mercy keep them.
She weeps for all she could not give
But knows their Heavenly Father

Provided all so that they could live
And grow and go much further.
Know that you stand strong today
Because you stand upon her prayers.
Honour that always, come what may
And the Lord will give you favour.

Women of Zion

Women of Zion
We've gotta keep marching on
Through trials and sorrow
We sing redemption songs
Trusting in the Lord's Amazing Grace
We push forward with unshakeable faith
Women of Zion
We've gotta keep marching on

We are marching forwards
Because God has called us
Sisters of the most high
Anointed for His purpose
There's work to be done
Strongholds to break down
Daughters of the king
Taking trophies from the enemy's ground

Don't let your faith waver
We must stand together
'Cause iron sharpens iron
Let's pray and strengthen one another
As we march

Women of Zion
We've gotta keep marching on
Through trials and sorrow
We sing redemption songs
Trusting in the Lord's Amazing Grace
We push forward with unshakeable faith
Women of Zion
We've gotta keep marching on

We are marching onwards
The enemy can't stop us
Chosen of the King
Pressing for the prize before us
We are glory-bound
Can't you hear the sound
Of those who came before us
Whose faithfulness has ploughed this ground

We may cry sometimes
There will be pain sometimes
But the peace and love of God
Is the rock under which we hide
As we march

Women of Zion
We've gotta keep marching on
Through trials and sorrow
We sing redemption songs
Trusting in the Lord's Amazing Grace
We push forward with unshakeable faith
Women of Zion
We've gotta keep marching on

We are sold out
We are called out
To preach the gospel of the Lord
That's what this living's all about

Women of the Lord
Take up your shield and sword
Yes, the battle is hot,
        but we know the victory shall be ours

Women of the Lord
Take up your shield and sword

Yes, the battle is hot,
        but we know the victory shall be ours

Women of Zion
We've gotta keep marching on
Through trials and sorrow
We sing redemption songs
Trusting in the Lords Amazing Grace
We push forward with unshakeable faith
Women of Zion
We've gotta keep marching on

Love Letter

Dear Lord,

I love You
Because You saw something good in me
Because You healed the scars no one else could see
Because You give me Your joy for all my pain
Because of You I can live again

I love You
Because Your Word steadies me when I falter
Because You turn my tears into healing water
Because when I am weak, You are perfectly strong
Because Your presence is where my heart belongs

I love You
Because You gave me beauty for my ashes
Because You're my safe harbour when the storm crashes
Because You give my life purpose every day
Because You ear is tuned to my heart when I pray

I love You
Because You love me just as I am
Because in the face of the enemy,
        You give me courage to stand
Because Your promises are a balm to my soul
Because You took these broken pieces
        and You made them whole

I love You
Because Your arms enfold me in my fear of the night
Because You stir my soul and restore my sight
Because You always do what You say You will do
Because no earthly love would prove as true

Because You take my best and You make it better
I just had to write You this love letter.

Heart Physician

I gave my heart away once;
    to someone I thought was true
They took it, and they used it;
    gave it back to me so battered and bruised
Until every fragile heartbeat
    would only make me cry
My heart hurt so badly within me
    I thought that I would die
I thought there was no remedy
    for these shattered, broken pieces
Until I knelt in prayer one day
    and called on the name of Jesus.
Then suddenly I felt the clouds
    of pain begin to part
And I felt the gentle hand of God
    as he healed my broken heart.

So, I stand here to testify
    to all who are in pain
Who think their shattered, broken heart
    will never be whole again
That there is a God in heaven
    who sees each tear that falls
Who is always waiting patiently,
    if you would only call
He will take you in His arms
    and love the hurt away
To give you strength and courage
    to love another day.
If you can learn to trust Him,
    then He can make a start
So, call on the only physician
    that can heal the broken heart.

FINALE

My Soul in Healing and Triumph

For whosever is born of God overcometh the world: and this is the victory that overcometh the world, even our faith.

1 John 5:4

TESTIMONIES HAVE POWER; POWER TO MOVE, TO change, convict the spirit. There is nothing so convincing as reliable personal witness. Testimonies tell people about the journey we have travelled to arrive at our current destination. It doesn't mean the journey is complete, but it gives a picture of the hope we have as we continue. There is an old song that has the line, "I don't believe He brought me this far to leave me." Philippians 1:6 says, "...being confident of this very thing, that He which began a good work in you will be faithful to perform it until the day of Jesus Christ." Too many times, however, we hold on to our testimony because we are waiting for the final victory. We must understand that the final victory is when we overcome death and the grave and are risen again with Jesus. Until then, we will rise and fall and rise again. Micah 7:8 states, "Rejoice not against me, O mine enemy: when I fall, I shall arise; when I sit in darkness, the Lord shall be a light unto me." This is my victory. This is my healing. This is my hope. Despite all the battles, I am still here. When I have been low enough to consider suicide, the Lord has allowed me to arise. As far as I have fallen, God has picked me up again and again. He remains faithful. He is always merciful.

Healing does not mean that suddenly all pain is gone; that there are no days when I do not feel low and tired and overwhelmed. Even as I am writing this, I am fighting those feelings. Healing comes in many forms. When I am at peace, when I can feel God's presence despite everything that is going on in my mind, in my body and in my soul, I am healed by that presence. When I am weak, my healing comes in knowing that God is my strength and through Him I can do anything. The limitations of my mind and my body do not prevent me from being a witness of God's greatness, God's mercy, God's grace. Every day that I overcome those struggles, it is a testimony of what God is doing in me and through me. When others with mental health issues see me talking, preaching, performing or simply living day to day, it is a witness of what is possible through God; it is testimony to the fact that the demons don't win and that I can overcome.

But, as always, the beginning and the ending intertwine. How can anyone understand my testimony, the joy, the elation I express, without any understanding of the struggle? How can our testimony really have any power unless people know what we have had to overcome to be here?

These last few poems are about being victorious. They are about knowing that we can stand on the Word of God even when the world seems to be in turmoil. They celebrate the fact that no matter what I am going through, my life is abundant because my life is in Jesus. They let others know the joy, love, peace and sense of freedom there is in God and they speak of the peace of God that calms me when my soul is in turmoil.

My victory and healing in Jesus is the centre of my truth, because I know that every day that I stand, it is because He has given me the strength to do so. Every victory is because of His grace and His mercy. Every testimony is about His greatness, His forgiveness, His mercy, His everlasting love. I am one of them "which came out of great tribulation and have washed their robes and made them white in the blood of the lamb" (Revelation 7:14). We overcome by the blood of the Lamb and by the word of our testimony (Revelation 12:11).

This is my testimony; this is my truth; this is all my naked soul.

The Morning

The night is almost over
The day is almost here;
Time to put away your worry
Time to put away your fear.

Time to face the morning sunlight
With a heart that's free and true.
See that open door before you?
It's time to step on through.

Time to put away old anger
Lay the pangs of pain to death
Time to cleanse away the shadows
With a deep, clear, open breath.

Time to silence the swirling whispers
That corrode your fledging hope;
Stop looking to enemies for rescue
Stop clinging to fragile, broken rope.

Time to embrace the God within you
Time to wake and face the light
Know His peace and joy are with you
Your morning's dawning bright.

Treasures

I did not know myself.
I defined myself by their labels;
I was the me I thought I should be.

Now I see myself reflected in your friendship;
You have gifted me with new names,
They pour down on me like rain on roses.
I blossom and grow.
I am nourished and sustained.

I see treasure where once I only saw fool's gold

You are my family.
The ties that bind are less tangible
But more secure than blood and veins.
They hold tightly and do not let go.
They pull me back from the shadows of loneliness.
They see my flaws and know they make me human.

I reciprocate.

I love you in all your imperfections;
I see your treasure, your beauty.
When you cannot see yourself clearly
I hold up my friendship as a mirror
So that you can come back to yourself.

We are fearfully and wonderfully made;
My sister,
My friend.

Unshakable

Everything changes.

Standing beside an unyielding grave
That has swallowed a loved one
Too soon,
Too hurt, too much, tears mingle with the dust
To which they have returned
As we all must.
Still it feels
As though the world tilts, tilts on its axis
Spinning round and round
Everyone grappling for solid ground;

And they wonder how we still stand.

Everything changes.

When silent hope fades
When the job for life vanished yesterday
The call of the creditors bawl and bay
As all that you'd saved for a rainy day
Spills down the draw of pain and sorrow
Of that unexpected tomorrow
That has you feeling
As though the world tilts, tilts on its axis
Spinning round and round
Everyone grappling for solid ground;

And they wonder how we still stand.

Everything changes.

When the one that whispered love
Vowed, but could not pay

Shatters the sanctity of the home
Then calmly walks away,
It seems that there are no pieces to put together
Only fair-weather friends
Who cannot stand with you till the bitter end;
But shrug their shoulders and shake their heads
Roll over in their own uncomfortable beds
While your world seems to tilt, tilt on its axis
Spinning round and round
Everyone grappling for solid ground;

They wonder how we can still stand.

Everything changes.

In a politician's sound bite
That promises everything will be alright
Whilst nightmare scenes scream daily
        on our television screens
Burning the glib words
As towns, cities, countries melt into dust
Man-made rubble of discord and distrust
Blood, sweat, tears on the face of an innocent
Who just doesn't get it
Who doesn't understand
Why the world seems to tilt, tilt on its axis
Spinning round and round
Everyone grappling for solid ground;

And they wonder why we still stand.

Everything changes.

In the squeeze of a psychotic trigger
That's bigger than the bravado of a young man's knife
Both leeching life on to territorial streets
Uncaring, unknowing of the mothers' cry

Who struggles to understand why
The world seems to tilt, tilt on its axis
Spinning round and round
Everyone grappling for solid ground.

Everything changes
Yet, here we stand
On this rock
Unmovable, unshakeable, always ready
Through the storm, His hand holding us steady
His name a constant praise
Every prayer a weapon in the fight
Marching on this rock
Surrounded by a heavenly army day and night
And the world is looking, as their world is tilting.
When their world went spinning they tripped and fell
It spun their soul closer to hell
They don't know it, but they're looking for rescue
They just don't know the answer
But we do.
So, someone sound the battle cry
"On Christ, the solid rock I stand"
Let's march into battle
Let's take back this land
Snatching souls from the enemy,
Who with unholy glee
Wants to rob them of heaven
And rob you and me
Of our peace and our joy and our heavenly crown
But his weapons won't work if we take a stand
As the world seems to tilt, tilt on its axis,
Spinning round and round.
Children of God,
Stand!

Evangelism in Rhyme

Give me one minute
Just a minute of your time
One minute; I'll make it worth your while
I want to make it clear
That I am not here
To judge you
Or make you feel bad about yourself
Life does that to us all
All by itself
I'm not here to point out the flaws
That exist in us all
Or draw a road map to your pain
Not to expose the rawness of your pretence
Or tear down that barbed wire fence
You've built around your heart
I want to talk about love
His love
That already has your brokenness
Bound in His sacrifice
Love that understands your hurt
Because He felt it
Love that wants you to know at the cross,
    He already dealt with it
Love that sees behind
The screen of our silence
That hears the scream that no one else notices
So please
I'm only asking for a minute
Sixty seconds
To speak about the blessings you have been missing
I'm not talking about the singing and the shouting
That's not what I'm about
In fact
That's a by-product of His love, an overflow

That fertilises the spirit and helps it grow
I don't even want to talk about the need and the greed
Of a world that doesn't see you
But only values what you do
In exchange for your soul
Instead, I want to talk about a love
　　　that can make you whole
See, I know you've been searching
　　　and you've been seeking
Thought you found it in someone's arms
But it left your soul raw and bleeding
So you've exchanged love for sex
Locked your heart in a cell
But if you just search a little deeper
You will find a well
Waiting to spring into a fountain
　　　of love and joy and peace
Wash away the past and give you release
That's His love
It makes you complete
Just a few more seconds
Before you go
Just a little while longer to let you know
That there's no condemnation
I've been where you've been
And no, I'm not perfect
But His love keeps me free
So I don't have to worry about the stress and the strain
I just give it all to Him
When I call on His name
And I'm overwhelmed by a love
　　　that I can't always explain
I just have to share it
Though you might turn away
And dismiss me as some fanatic with nothing to say
But if you have heard and you can believe
In His love and His Mercy

He will receive
All that you are, no matter how broken
Thank you for your patience
My minute is over.

Faith (Now is the Time)

Now
Is the
Time
To silence
Fear
To shut out
Doubt

Now
Is the
Time
To push
Past the
Ordinary
To step
Beyond the
Possible

Now
Is the
Time
To reach
Towards
That elusive
Dream

Now
Is the
Time
To run
Faster
To climb
Higher

Right
Now
This
Moment
Is the
Time
To ride the
Supernova
To the
Excellence
Of your
Being
And become
The magic
In your
Soul

God's Peace

He comes to me on a summer breeze
That whispers love and gives me peace
That soothes my soul and mends my heart
And bids all lingering fears depart
He comes to me in a shower of rain
That washes away past hurt and pain
That cleanses me from deep within
And reminds me that I belong to Him.

Abundant Life

You think you know what you see
When you see me
I see the way you look and shake your head
As though I were a book you've already read
Entitled 'The God Delusion 'or 'The Fanatical Fool'
Or some other label that suits the mood
Of a generation that would rather
Live vicariously through other people's drama

But I am fearfully and wonderfully made
By a God who knew me when I was substance
Designed me for a purpose
So, I propose
That if you're a hater
You take it up with the Creator of all things
Who has called me by my name
And knows that in my small, slim frame
I am obese with creativity
Words and music combine in the rhythm of my walk
And images and dreams flow through me when I talk

You think my pain is a game I play
To which you have made up the rules
Thinking you can use them to bind me in chains
But through my God I can leap over walls
Stride through the giant of your small mind
While my visions leave you behind
Down on your knees,
Reeling in the dust
While I march on, strong in the God that I trust

You think I believe in some deluded reality
You don't understand my worship,
    so you question my sanity

May I suggest you stop focusing on me
Start dealing with your own insecurities
Tear down the skewed mirrors
That tell you that a lighter life
        is only a slimming world away
That life is only worth what you can afford to pay.
Strip away the mask that pretends that you're loving it
When it is leaking silicone through your scattered dreams
Because the body of your life is not what it seems

I don't need to join your commercial revolution
I was reborn into the real solution

You see, I already know the truth
I'm living it
If you want to be a cynic that's up to you
Talk is cheap, so talk as much as you want to

As for me; I'm living life abundantly.

Appendix 1

Panic and Anxiety Disorder

Panic disorder is an anxiety disorder in which you regularly have sudden attacks of panic or fear.

Everyone experiences feelings of anxiety and panic at certain times. It's a natural response to stressful or dangerous situations. But for someone with panic disorder, feelings of anxiety, stress and panic occur regularly and at any time, often for no apparent reason.

Symptoms of Anxiety

Anxiety is a feeling of unease. It can range from mild to severe and can include feelings of worry and fear. The most severe form of anxiety is panic. You may start to avoid certain situations because you fear they'll trigger another attack. This can create a cycle of living 'in fear of fear'. It can add to your sense of panic and may cause you to have more attacks.

Symptoms of Panic Attacks

A panic attack is when your body experiences a rush of intense mental and physical symptoms. It can come on very quickly and for no apparent reason. A panic attack can be very frightening and distressing. This can include: a racing heartbeat, feeling faint, sweating, nausea, chest pain, shortness of breath, trembling, hot flushes, chills, shaky limbs, a choking sensation, dizziness, numbness, a need to go to the toilet, ringing in your ears, a feeling of dread or a fear of dying, a churning stomach, a tingling sensation in your fingers, feeling like you're not connected to your body.

Most panic attacks last for between five and twenty minutes. Some panic attacks have been reported to last up to an hour. The number of attacks you have will depend on how severe your condition is. Some people have attacks once or twice a month, while others have them several times a week. Although panic attacks are frightening, they're not dangerous. An attack won't cause you any physical harm, and it's unlikely that you'll be admitted to hospital if you have one.

Be aware that most of these symptoms can also be symptoms of other conditions or problems, so you may not always be experiencing a panic attack – for example, you may have a racing heartbeat if you have very low blood pressure.

Causes

As with many mental health conditions, the exact cause of panic disorder isn't fully understood. But it's thought the condition is probably linked to a combination of things, including:

- a traumatic or very stressful life experience, such as bereavement;
- having a close family member with the disorder;
- an imbalance of neurotransmitters (chemical messengers) in the brain.

Appendix 2

Fibromyalgia

Fibromyalgia, also called fibromyalgia syndrome (FMS), is a long-term condition that causes pain all over the body.

The exact cause of fibromyalgia is unknown, but it's thought to be related to abnormal levels of certain chemicals in the brain and changes in the way the central nervous system (brain, spinal cord and nerves) processes pain messages carried around the body.

Widespread Pain

If you have fibromyalgia, one of the main symptoms is likely to be widespread pain. This may be felt throughout your body, but could be worse in some areas, such as your back or neck. The pain is likely to be continuous, although it may be better or more severe at different times. The pain could feel like an ache; a burning sensation; a sharp, stabbing pain.

Extreme Sensitivity

Fibromyalgia can make you extremely sensitive to pain all over your body, and you may find that even the slightest touch is painful. If you hurt yourself – such as stubbing your toe – the pain may continue for much longer than it normally would. You may hear the condition described in the following medical terms: hyperalgesia – when you're extremely sensitive to pain; allodynia – when you feel pain from something that shouldn't be painful at all, such as a very light touch. You may also be sensitive to things such as smoke, certain foods and bright lights. Being exposed to something you're sensitive to can cause your other fibromyalgia symptoms to flare up.

Stiffness

Fibromyalgia can make you feel stiff. The stiffness may be most severe when you've been in the same position for a long period of time – for example, when you first wake up in the morning. It can also cause your muscles to spasm, which is when they contract (squeeze) tightly and painfully.

Fatigue

Fibromyalgia can cause fatigue (extreme tiredness). This can range from a mild tired feeling to the exhaustion often experienced during a flu-like illness. Severe fatigue may come on suddenly and can drain you of all your energy. If this happens, you may feel too tired to do anything at all.

Poor Sleep Quality

Fibromyalgia can affect your sleep. You may often wake up tired, even when you've had plenty of sleep. This is because the condition can sometimes prevent you from sleeping deeply enough to refresh you properly. You may hear this described as 'non-restorative sleep'.

Cognitive Problems ('Fibro-Fog')

Cognitive problems are issues related to mental processes, such as thinking and learning. If you have fibromyalgia, you may have trouble remembering and learning new things; problems with attention and concentration; slowed or confused speech.

Headaches

If fibromyalgia has caused you to experience pain and stiffness in your neck and shoulders, you may also have frequent headaches. These can vary from being mild headaches to severe migraines, and could also involve other symptoms, such as nausea (feeling sick).

Irritable Bowel Syndrome (IBS)

Some people with fibromyalgia also develop irritable bowel syndrome (IBS). IBS is a common digestive condition that causes pain and bloating in your stomach. It can also lead to constipation or diarrhoea.

Other Symptoms

Dizziness and clumsiness, feeling too hot or too cold – this is because you're not able to regulate your body temperature properly, restless legs syndrome (an overwhelming urge to move your legs), tingling, numbness, prickling or burning sensations in your hands and feet (pins and needles, also known as paraesthesia), in women, unusually painful periods, anxiety, depression.

Appendix 3

Help and Support

ANXIETY UK
www.anxietyuk.org.uk
Text Service: 07537 416 905

NO PANIC
www.nopanic.org.uk
Helpline: 0844 967 4848

TRIUMPH OVER PHOBIA (TOP UK)
www.topuk.org
Address: PO Box 3760, Bath, BA2 3WY, United Kingdom

FIBROMYALGIA UK
www.fmauk.org
National Helpline: 0300 999 3333

SAMARITANS
www.samatitans.org
Helpline: 116 123

MIND
www.mind.org.uk
Helpline: 0300 123 3393

CALM
www.thecalmzone.net
Helpline: 0800 58 58 58

THE SILVER LINE
www.thesilverline.org.uk
Helpline for Older People: 0800 4 70 80 90

Similar Books by the Publisher

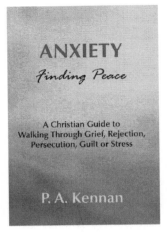

Anxiety – Finding Peace
P.A. Kennan

ISBN 978-1-78815-708-7

The principles that Kennan teaches in this book help tackle the anxiety that can arise from unforeseen circumstances, such as the loss of loved one through death or divorce, or rejection/bullying from people we know. They also provide light at the end of the tunnel when carrying feelings of guilt of shame. Find not just temporary relief, but a peace that lasts.

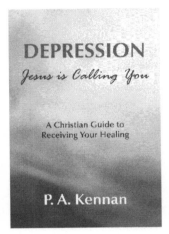

Depression – Jesus is Calling You
P.A. Kennan

ISBN 978-1-78815-665-3

Kennan summarises the known causes and common treatments of depression, then guides the reader through the relevant emotional and spiritual issues, providing practical insight that can lead towards recovery. Helpful for both those suffering from any level of depression, as well as a useful resource for counselling, this holistic guide provides a biblical, Christian perspective on current medical understanding.

Books available from all good bookshops and from the publisher:
www.onwardsandupwards.org